I0064498

Transitions

LIZETTE IBARRA

Transitions

©Copyright 2025, Lizette Ibarra.
All rights reserved.

No portion of this book may be reproduced by mechanical, photographic, or electronic process; nor may it be stored in a retrieval system, transmitted in any form, or otherwise be copied for public use or private use without written permission of the copyright owner.

It is sold with the understanding that the publisher and the individual author are not engaged in the rendering of psychological, legal, accounting, or other professional advice.

The content and views in this book are the sole expression and opinion of the author and not necessarily the views of Fig Factor Media, LLC.

For More Information:

Fig Factor Media | figfactormedia.com
Lizette Ibarra | www.itslizette.com

Cover Design & Layout by LDG Juan Manuel Serna Rosales

Printed in the United States of America

ISBN: 978-1-961600-61-4

FIG FACTOR MEDIA

DEDICATION

To Alex, my life partner of twenty-five years and counting—thank you for every transition we've embraced together.

To my changos—Diego and Valeria—you are my greatest transformation and joy.

TABLE OF CONTENTS

TRANSITIONS, EVEN THE HARDEST ONES, ARE NOT JUST HAPPENING TO YOU; THEY'RE HAPPENING FOR YOU.

_____

TO EVERY READER,
THANK YOU FOR
ALLOWING ME TO BE
PART OF YOUR JOURNEY.
MAY THIS BOOK
OFFER YOU INSIGHTS,
COURAGE, AND HOPE
AS YOU EMBRACE
THE OPPORTUNITIES
THAT PROFESSIONAL
TRANSITIONS BRING.

_____

ACKNOWLEDGMENTS

—

Writing this book has been a journey of reflection and deep gratitude. It would not have been possible without the incredible individuals who have trusted and supported me throughout my own professional journey.

To the hundreds, maybe thousands, of professionals and leaders I've had the privilege to interview and guide—thank you for sharing your unique and precious stories. One of the greatest lessons I've learned is that our professional lives are not just "work." They are catalysts for our purpose, shaping who we are and what we value. They allow us to provide for our families, experience freedom and joy, or face profound challenges like disappointment and burnout.

The changes and transitions we experience in our careers can be profoundly transformative. Whether navigating the disappointment of rejection, venturing into entrepreneurship, or redefining a career path later in life, these moments are far more than professional shifts—they are life transitions that touch every aspect of who we are.

I am profoundly grateful for my tribe—my colleagues, mentors, team, clients, partner organizations, and collaborators. Thank you for your trust, your belief in me, and your unwavering support. Each of you has played an integral role in shaping the professional and personal journey that led to this book.

INTRODUCTION:
Why Transitions Matter

—

Transitions are universal, yet deeply personal. When we face them—especially the tough ones—they can feel isolating, overwhelming, and even disorienting. Whether it's an exciting promotion, a career pivot, or an unexpected job loss, professional transitions often challenge more than just our work lives. They ripple through our well-being, our families, and even our sense of identity.

Change is external—a job loss, a move, a shift in a relationship, or even aging. Transition, however, is internal. It's the emotional and psychological process we go through to adapt to those changes. And it's this process—messy, nonlinear, and deeply personal—that shapes who we become on the other side.

Work is not just a 9-to-5. It's a source of purpose, connection, and fulfillment. A job can make us incredibly happy or unbearably miserable. It shapes how we see ourselves and how others see us. Professional transitions, in particular, force us to confront our fears, question our paths, and find new ways to grow. They're not just about the roles we leave behind or step into—they're about who we become along the way.

Even what seems like a joyful transition—like landing a big promotion or starting a dream job—can bring its own challenges, such as imposter syndrome, fear of failure, or struggling to balance new responsibilities. And tougher transitions, like leaving a toxic workplace or facing an unexpected layoff, can feel like a blow to our very core. But in both cases, transitions make us more human. They push us to reflect, to adapt, and ultimately to transform.

Transitions aren't happening to you; they're happening for you. They provide a unique opportunity to grow, redefine success, and craft a future aligned with your values and aspirations. In this book, we'll delve into some of the most common—and often challenging—career transitions. Let's embark on this transformative journey together.

CHAPTER 1:
Phases of Transition

Transitions are rarely straightforward. They are deeply personal journeys that unfold in phases, each bringing unique challenges and opportunities for growth. Understanding these phases can provide clarity and resilience as we navigate the uncertainty.

The first phase, **Endings,** a phase of life as we knew it, marks the beginning of every transition. It involves letting go of what once was—a job, a role, or an identity. Endings can feel like loss, evoking emotions such as sadness, anger, or relief. Yet, they are necessary to create space for what comes next.

From endings, we step into **Uncertainty,** a phase that can be accompanied by fear or excitement, reflects the complexity of transitions. Even exciting changes, such as a job promotion or relocation to a new country, often bring uncertainty and the pressure to succeed. On the other hand, deeply challenging transitions, like job loss or burnout, can evoke fear and doubt. This phase invites us to confront the unknown, trust ourselves, and explore new possibilities. It is characterized by discomfort and doubt as we grapple with the unknown. It is natural to feel unsteady, but this phase invites us to trust ourselves and explore new possibilities.

Acceptance follows as we release resistance and embrace the reality of change. These transitions can take months or years, challenging us to surrender while also shaping the process intentionally. The key lies in questioning our inner selves: What do we truly want? What lessons can we learn? This introspection transforms uncertainty into clarity.

Next comes **The Gifts,** where growth, insights, and unexpected opportunities emerge. Transitions reveal strengths and perspectives we didn't know we had, moving us closer to the person we are becoming.

Finally, we arrive at **New Beginnings,** where the transformation takes place. This phase is about stepping into a new chapter with purpose and renewed confidence.

Transitions are not just events but evolutions. Understanding these phases allows us to navigate them with grace, courage, and hope.

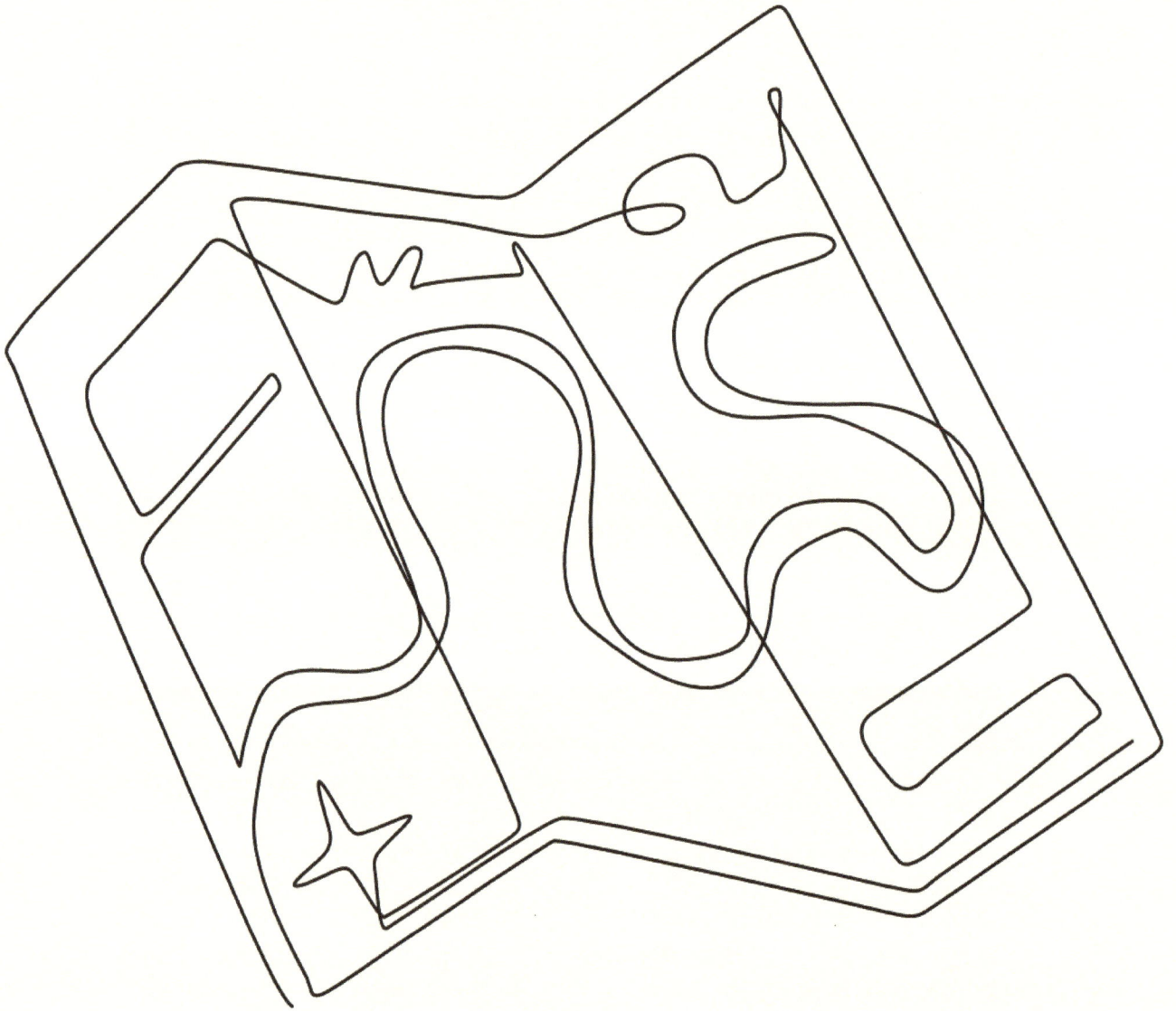

CHAPTER 2:
How to Put Yourself into a 'Transition' Mindset

―

Transition begins in the mind. While change is an external event or circumstance that alters your environment, transition is the internal process of adapting to that change. Embracing a "transition" mindset is key to navigating these moments with resilience and purpose. This chapter will guide you in shifting your perspective to approach transitions as opportunities rather than obstacles.

Reframe your thinking. This first step recognizes that transitions are not happening to you but for you. This shift in perspective helps reduce resistance and fosters acceptance. Rather than focusing solely on what you've lost, ask yourself: What can I gain from this experience? What lessons might emerge from this process?

Feeling overwhelmed? Break it into smaller, manageable steps. Focus on what you can control today. Seek support from trusted individuals who can help you find a way forward. Even the most profound transitions start with small acts of courage.

Cultivate self-awareness. Transitions require you to confront your inner beliefs, fears, and aspirations. Take time to reflect on your values and priorities. Journaling or speaking with a trusted confidant can help uncover patterns and clarify what truly matters.

Practice patience and self-compassion. Transitions are journeys, not races. Allow yourself to feel the emotions that arise, whether they are fear, excitement, or uncertainty. Remember, growth often requires discomfort.

Set intentions, not rigid goals. While goals can feel overwhelming during times of upheaval, intentions provide flexibility and focus. Consider what kind of person you want to become through this transition and let that guide your actions.

Embrace curiosity and adaptability. Finally, transitions are ripe with opportunities to explore new paths and redefine success. By staying open and adaptable, you can uncover possibilities you never imagined.

A transition mindset doesn't eliminate challenges, but it empowers you to navigate them with confidence and clarity, transforming uncertainty into growth.

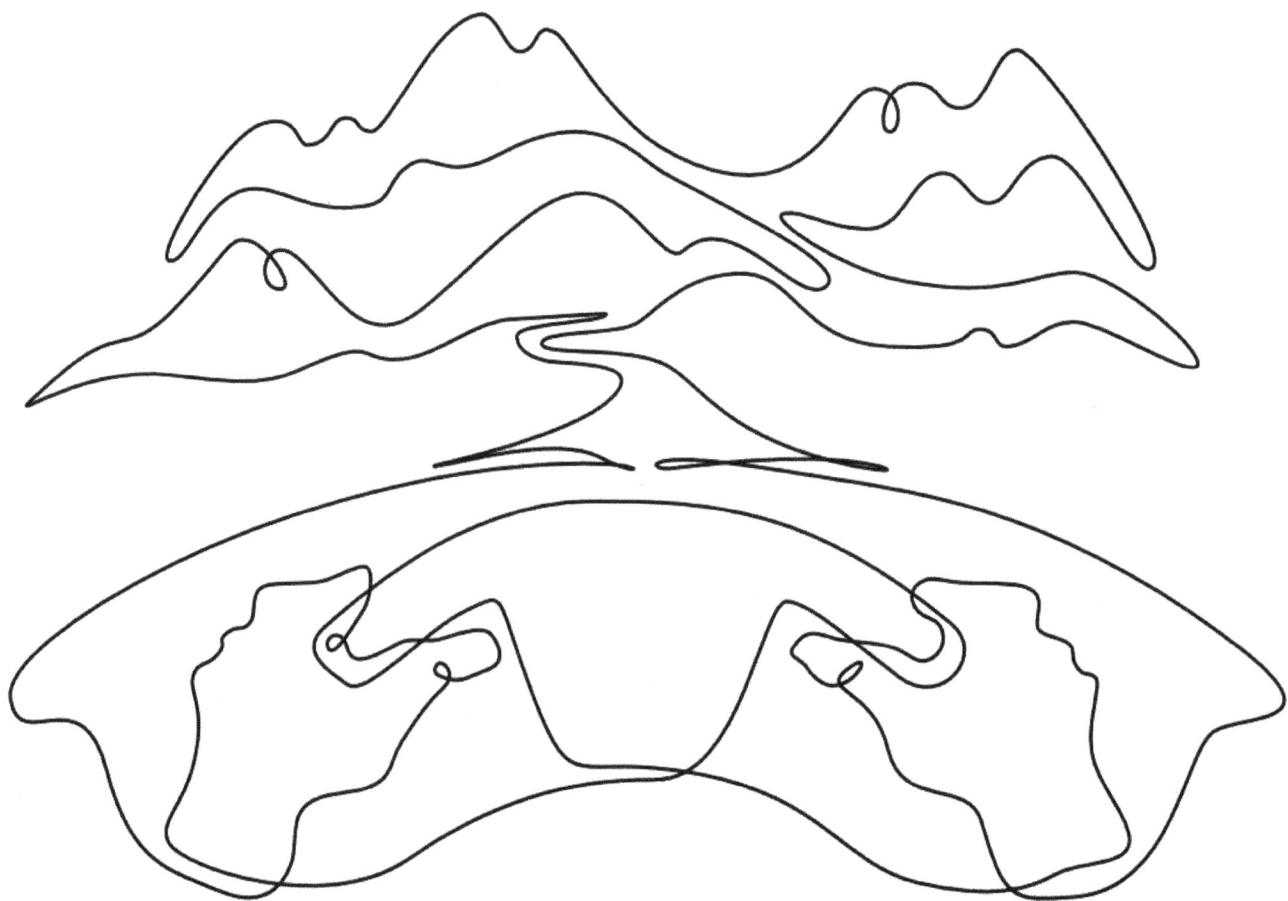

CHAPTER 3:
Shifting from Corporate to Entrepreneurship

Becoming an entrepreneur was never part of my plan. I loved my corporate career and had dreams of becoming a chief human resources officer (CHRO) or a chief executive officer (CEO) in a global corporation. But when I became a mother, balancing a demanding job and raising my son without a support system, became overwhelming. I made the difficult decision to step back from corporate life and explore a new path.

At first, it was just me, a pen, and a notebook in a spare room where I could work while caring for my son. The uncertainty was immense, but I gave myself grace to manage it one day at a time. There were awful days filled with doubt, but I focused on small wins. Each tiny success fueled my determination.

As time went on, I began to embrace the freedom and possibilities that entrepreneurship offered. Slowly, I grew my business and created opportunities not just for myself but for others. I brought women like me—mothers who had taken a break and couldn't find a way back—into my growing search firm.

This wasn't just a career shift—it was a profound transition. Without realizing it, I was adapting to change and transforming into a whole new version of myself. I learned to embrace uncertainty, to trust the process, and to allow the journey to shape me. Transitions thrive on grace, small wins, and the courage to build something meaningful from change.

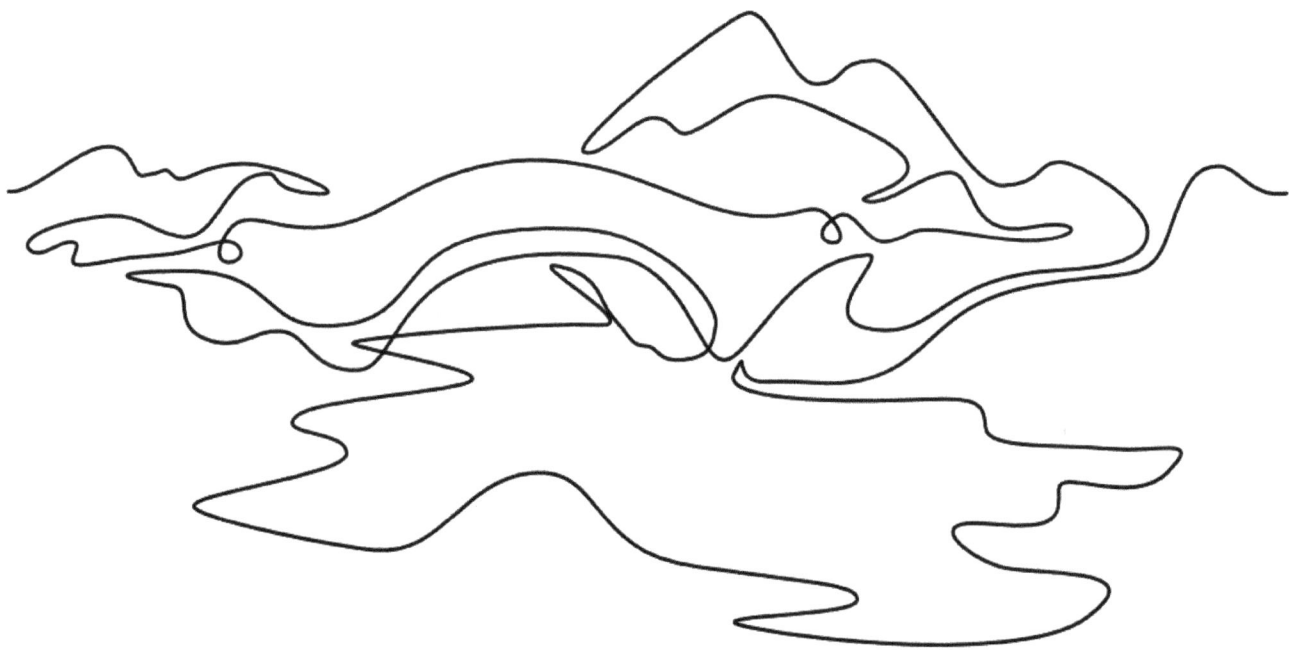

CHAPTER 4:
Coping with the Disappointment of Not Getting the Dream Job

Rejection stings. Pouring your hopes into a dream job, only to be turned away, feels deeply personal. The disappointment often feels like a judgment on your worth. And yes—it hurts.

But here's what I always tell candidates, not getting that job doesn't mean there's something wrong with you. You might be the perfect candidate for one organization but not for another. Every company has unique needs, cultures, and nuances. Often, it's the smallest detail—not a reflection of your talent—that determines the outcome.

This is where the difference between change and transition becomes crucial. Not getting the job is a sudden, external event. Transition is the internal process of reframing, adapting, and moving forward. While the change feels immediate, the transition takes time and intention.

One key to navigating disappointment is to never rely solely on Plan A. Having a Plan B, C, or even D prepares you for setbacks and opens the door to unexpected opportunities. Rejection may feel like the end, but it's often a blessing in disguise, redirecting you to something better suited to your values and aspirations.

Start by giving yourself grace to feel the disappointment. Then, take small steps forward—reflect on the process, refine your approach, and stay open to new paths.

Remember, rejection isn't failure—it's redirection. Your worth isn't tied to one opportunity, and transitions hold the power to transform. Trust that something even better is waiting for you.

CHAPTER 5:
When the Unexpected Happens: Navigating Job Loss

Out of all professional transitions, an unexpected job loss stings the most. It's not just about losing a paycheck—it's about losing stability, identity, and a sense of purpose. For those with long tenures, ascending careers, or leadership roles, the impact is even greater. It strikes at the core of your ego, leaving you questioning your value and place in the world.

Throughout my career, I've spoken to countless executives who've faced this moment. They describe it as a profound loss, almost like grieving a loved one. The first and most pressing thought often is, *How do I tell my family?* The weight of this news, combined with the shame many feel—even though it isn't deserved—makes returning home almost unbearable.

Why does it feel so personal? Because losing a job isn't just about work. It's about walking away from the relationships you've built, the routine that grounds you, and the sense of belonging that comes from being part of an organization. Packing your desk, saying goodbyes, and walking out with a box is more than symbolic—it's an emotional experience that shakes you to your core.

So, if you find yourself in this position—unexpectedly losing your job—hear me out, you are not alone. You are not the first, nor will you be the last. Even icons, like Steve Jobs, were once let go. In his own words, *"I didn't see it then, but it turned out that getting fired from Apple was the best thing that could have ever happened to me. The heaviness of being successful was replaced by the lightness of being a beginner again, less sure about everything. It freed me to enter one of the most creative periods of my life."* [1]

---
[1] *Steve Jobs, 2005 commencement address at Stanford University*

CHAPTER 5:
Continued...

Losing your job has nothing to do with your worth as a person or professional. It's a reminder that no one is indispensable in the corporate world, no matter how accomplished or irreplaceable you might feel. (Read that twice.)

The key is to recognize that while losing a job is a sudden and external change, the real work lies in the transition—the internal process of adapting, reframing, and finding new meaning. Yes, it hurts. Yes, it's scary. But transitions hold the potential for incredible growth.

Start by allowing yourself to grieve the loss. It's okay to feel sad, angry, or overwhelmed. These emotions are valid and necessary to move forward. Next, shift your perspective. What doors might this unexpected turn open? What opportunities could emerge? Life's detours often lead to paths we couldn't have planned ourselves.

Finally, trust the process. Embrace the uncertainty, lean into the discomfort, and stay open to transformation. One day, you may look back at this moment with gratitude, recognizing it as the catalyst for a new and fulfilling chapter.

CHAPTER 6:
Returning to Work After Motherhood

This chapter hits close to home for me. As I shared in Chapter 3, I became an entrepreneur because balancing corporate life with motherhood felt impossible. But before that, I did return to corporate for a full year after my first son, Diego, was born, and it changed me forever.

Motherhood draws a sharp line between life as you knew it and life as it will ever be. Your body changes, your mind shifts, and your heart grows in beautiful yet profoundly challenging ways. In Mexico, I had just forty-two days of maternity leave before I was expected back at work—laws almost certainly written by men who had no idea what a new mother endures.

I remember feeding my baby three times a night, surviving on fractured sleep, and heading to the office at 6:30 a.m. with a smile for daycare drop-off. My milk pump was my constant companion, a silent reminder of my dual roles. Meetings often became a physical battle, suppressing the urge to pump while focusing on work. Eventually, I hired a nanny, sacrificing 60 percent of my salary for the peace of mind that my baby could stay home while I worked.

Then there are stories like the woman I heard about recently. She secretly brought her aunt on a work trip to care for her baby at a nearby hotel, sneaking away every three to four hours to breastfeed. She told no one, carefully planning to attend the meeting and fulfill her responsibilities as a mother. When the meeting location changed last minute, she broke down, calling her boss late at night, embarrassed to reveal her situation. No one knew the lengths she had gone to just to make it work.

This story is a testament to the incredible challenges women face and the extraordinary lengths we go to in order to combine motherhood and work. Because yes, many of us love both. We cherish our children while finding fulfillment, independence, and purpose in our work. Yet, with every meeting, every trip, and every milestone missed, we carry the heavy weight of guilt.

The **change** is becoming a mom. The **transformation** is learning to reconcile these two worlds—knowing life and work will never look the same and finding the strength to adapt. Motherhood reshapes you, challenges you, and teaches you resilience. It's not about choosing one over the other but about finding imperfect ways to embrace both.

CHAPTER 7:
Pursuing a Career Change Later in Life

L et's get something straight, the days of a thirty-year career at the same company as the ultimate achievement are behind us. Decades ago, loyalty to one organization symbolized stability and success. But today, many of us feel a deeper call pulling us toward something different—whether it's entrepreneurship or an entirely new field. It's not just a change; it's a transition—a journey from where we are to where we're meant to be.

After fifteen or twenty years in the same field, it's natural to ask, *"Is this all there is?"* *"Could there be more waiting for me if I dared to try?"* A career change later in life can feel daunting because change is external—it's the shift from one role or field to another. But transition is internal—it's the emotional and psychological process of redefining your purpose, adapting to uncertainty, and embracing new possibilities.

I met someone who exemplifies this journey. She climbed to a vice president's role at one of the most prestigious Fortune 100 companies, earning seven figures. By all accounts, she was the definition of success. But inside, she felt an undeniable pull toward something more meaningful. After twenty-one years, she left corporate life to pursue her passion for executive coaching and public speaking. Was it easy? Absolutely not, she's had this internal struggle for years. But she had prepared for this transition by nurturing her passion alongside her career. My advice to anyone considering a career change later in life is this: Start early. Even if you're thriving in your corporate role, always have a Plan B. Cultivate a side hustle or a hobby that speaks to your passions. Even if it doesn't generate income at first, it plants seeds for the future.

Right now, as I write this, I'm feeling this pull myself. My career has been anything but boring—I've started four companies, launched seven brands, and embraced every twist and turn, including moving seven times. Yet, I feel this undeniable need inside of me to completely unleash my potential by merging one of my biggest passions in life with my professional journey.

Stay tuned, and together, we'll see how this transformation unfolds.

CHAPTER 8:
Moving on After a Major Setback

S etbacks are real, and they are particularly painful when they expose us. They shake our confidence, unearth vulnerabilities, and leave us feeling lost or judged. I read this recently: *"I am able to give advice not because I am smart, but because I have messed it up so many times."* These words resonate because setbacks often teach us more than success ever could.

Sometimes professional changes don't go as planned. Maybe you take a promotion before you're ready, only to struggle and lose the role. Or you leave a fulfilling job for what seems like a "dream opportunity," only to discover it's a poor fit. Perhaps you venture into entrepreneurship and face unexpected challenges. These moments are more than frustrating—they feel personal and disheartening.

Setbacks don't define you—they refine you. They provide clarity, build resilience, and offer lessons you can carry forward. The first step in moving on is to accept the discomfort and reflect on what went wrong. Learn from the experience, but don't dwell on it. Instead, focus on what you can control moving forward.

When you're ready, tell your story. Sharing your experience is liberating and can inspire others. Showing your vulnerability helps reframe the setback, transforming it into a meaningful part of your journey.

And yes, one day, what seems monumental now may feel smaller—perhaps even something you laugh about. Trust the process, rebuild with intention, and take it one step at a time. Setbacks are not the end. They are the beginning of a new, stronger chapter.

CHAPTER 9:
Burnout and Rediscovery

—

Burnout doesn't announce itself with a grand entrance. It creeps in slowly, like a fog that clouds your mind and weighs down your spirit. At first, you convince yourself it's just a rough patch—a busy season that will pass. But then, one day, you realize you've lost the spark. The joy, the passion, the drive that once propelled you forward—it's gone, leaving exhaustion and apathy in its place.

Burnout is more than just being tired. It's a profound disconnection from the work, people, or goals that once fueled you. It happens when the relentless pace of striving for success leaves no room for rest, reflection, or simply being. And while it feels like an end, burnout also can be a powerful catalyst for rediscovery.

The path to recovery doesn't begin with productivity hacks or pushing through. It begins with surrender—acknowledging that something is broken and needs healing. Give yourself permission to rest, to pause, and to reconnect with what truly matters. For some, this means stepping away from work entirely, even if only temporarily. For others, it means reevaluating priorities and saying "no" to what no longer serves them.

In burnout's aftermath lies an invitation to rediscover yourself. What excites you? What lights you up? What do you want your life to look like beyond the hustle? Often, burnout exposes the gaps between the life you're living and the one you truly desire. And this is when the gifts of this transformation and transition reveal themselves.

Rediscovery isn't an overnight process. It's a journey of small steps—choosing joy, setting boundaries, and reclaiming passions. With time, the spark returns, not as a flicker but as a steady flame. Burnout isn't the end; it's the beginning of a deeper, more intentional connection to yourself and to your purpose.

CHAPTER 10:
Shifting from Success to Significance: When to Stop Climbing

Success is often seen as the ultimate destination; a place we strive toward with relentless determination. But what happens when you're so busy climbing that you don't even realize you've arrived?

I've seen leaders get lost in the race for more—more titles, promotions, recognition. They forget to pause and ask, *"What does success mean for me?" "Am I living the life I once dreamed of?"*

When I was in my early thirties, I told myself I'd retire by forty. I imagined freedom and fulfillment. Yet here I am, far past that milestone, still striving for more. Why? Because success isn't static—it evolves. The real challenge is knowing when the pursuit becomes a cycle that no longer serves us.

I once asked a C-level executive—a leader working fourteen-hour days at the pinnacle of corporate success—if he felt successful. His hesitation said it all. He had been so consumed by the chase, he never paused to reflect on whether he was happy or fulfilled.

This is where **change** must lead to **transformation.** Success isn't about titles or income; it's about aligning with your values. Transformation begins when you stop chasing and start living—when you embrace your accomplishments and let them shape your next chapter.

For leaders, this means shifting from doing to being. Instead of asking, *"What's next?"* Ask, *"What truly matters now?"*

Success isn't a finish line. It's a journey that requires intentional pauses to redefine its meaning and ensure it serves your life—not the other way around.

CHAPTER 11:
Leaving a Toxic Workplace

———

Few things are as frustrating and demoralizing as being caught in a toxic workplace. The microaggressions, manipulation, and even outright disrespect can take a toll on your mental health and sense of self-worth. Toxicity from coworkers is bad enough, but when it comes from your boss, it cuts deeper, seeping into every corner of your professional and personal life.

I've seen people who love their work and feel a strong connection to their company's mission, service, or product. Yet, they're stuck in environments where toxicity drains their internal peace. When the source of that toxicity is your manager, it's even harder to navigate. You lie awake at night replaying every interaction, constantly on the defensive, unsure of what to expect next. You tell yourself to set boundaries, to fix the situation, but the harsh reality is this—when the toxicity comes from the top, it's unlikely to change.

So, what do you do? Do you stay and endure? Do you hope for a transfer to another department? Or do you make the choice to leave? The paycheck, your connection to the company, and the fear of the unknown often keep you stuck. But here's the truth, staying in a toxic environment can rob you of your confidence, health, and potential.

If you decide to leave, make it on your own terms, never as a reaction to a toxic act or situation—unless the situation crosses the boundaries of respect. Reach out to your network confidentially and begin exploring other opportunities in the market. Accept that, yes, sometimes life is unfair, and it might not be your fault that this is a toxic workplace, but it is your responsibility to find a better one where you can thrive.

The **change** is deciding to leave or finding a way out of the toxicity. The **transition** is the internal process of reclaiming your peace, finding clarity, and envisioning a healthier future. It's hard to walk away, but sometimes, leaving is the greatest act of self-preservation. Remember, you are not your job, and no role is worth your peace of mind. The transition might be uncomfortable, but on the other side is the chance to rebuild, grow, and rediscover your potential.

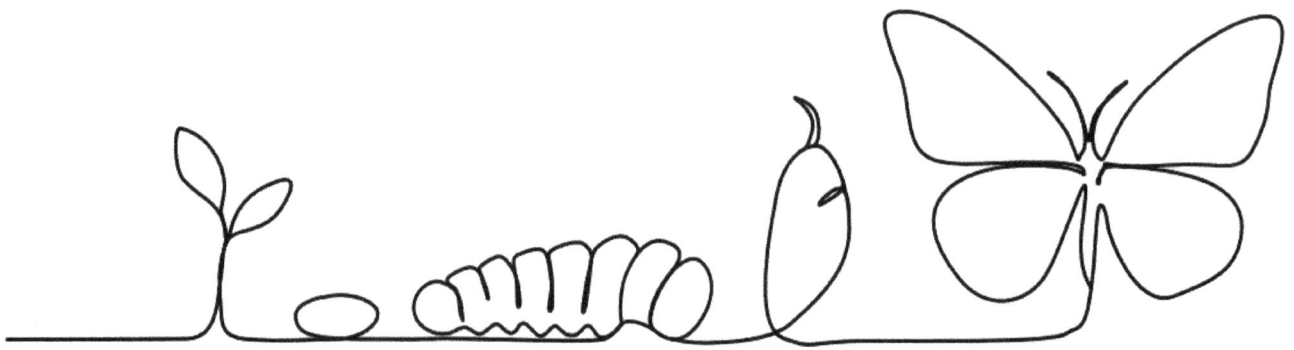

CHAPTER 12:
Conclusion

—

We often reflect on life transitions—getting married, divorced, graduating, or experiencing loss—but we sometimes overlook the profound impact professional transitions can have. They are no less transformative, no less challenging, and no less vital to shaping who we are.

Throughout this journey, I hope you've come to see that professional transitions are an inevitable part of life. They are not just about changing roles, industries, or locations—they are about growth, resilience, and discovering new dimensions of yourself. The more we embrace these moments and trust the process, the more we nurture our personal and professional evolution.

Whatever transition you're navigating right now, know this—you are not alone. You are not the first, and you will not be the last. But your journey is uniquely yours, and it's up to you to transform these changes into opportunities. Transitions challenge us to step outside our comfort zones, but they also invite us to reflect, to reinvent, and to rediscover what truly matters.

Through the setbacks, successes, uncertainties, and transformations, there are gifts—new perspectives, deeper connections, and a stronger, more authentic version of yourself waiting to emerge. Embrace these moments. Give yourself grace. When you're ready, tell your story. Sharing your experiences is liberating and inspiring, not just for you but for others who might be walking a similar path.

As I close this book, I am filled with gratitude—for the transitions I've faced, for the lessons they've taught me, and for the opportunity to share them with you. May you trust in your ability to adapt, to grow, and to thrive. **Remember, transitions, even the hardest ones, are not just happening TO you; they're happening FOR you.**

About the Author

Lizette Ibarra has spent more than twenty years as an entrepreneur in executive search, leadership consulting, and career strategy, and as a diversity, equity and inclusion expert. She has impacted many organizations by leading over 180 executive-level searches and facilitating the placement of more than 2,500 professionals. She specializes in talent attraction and retention as well as executive career transition and coaching.

As the visionary CEO and founder of Latina Chief, Lizette is dedicated to bridging the gender and ethnic leadership gaps and advocating for the advancement of women and Latinos in leadership roles. Serving on various boards, including the Hispanic Heritage Chamber of Commerce and United Latinas, she extends her influence to empower and support her community.

With a bachelor's degree in industrial relations and a master's degree in neuro-linguistic programming, Lizette brings a unique blend of academic knowledge and real-world experience to her work. She also holds certifications from prestigious institutions, including Harvard Business School and Cornell University, and is a Six Sigma champion.

Outside of her professional commitments, Lizette is a wife and mother, an accomplished tennis player, a skilled cook, and loves travel, good food, and wine. Based in Miami, Florida, she inspires and empowers others through her approach to leadership and life.

www.ingramcontent.com/pod-product-compliance
Lightning Source LLC
Chambersburg PA
CBHW050344230326
41458CB00102B/6354

9 781961 600614